ANIMAL BEHAVIOR

Horse Behavior

BY MARIE PEARSON

Kids Core
An Imprint of Abdo Publishing
abdobooks.com

abdobooks.com

Published by Abdo Publishing, a division of ABDO, PO Box 398166, Minneapolis, Minnesota 55439.

Printed in the United States of America, North Mankato, Minnesota.
052023
092023

THIS BOOK CONTAINS RECYCLED MATERIALS

Cover Photo: Rita Kochmarjova/Shutterstock Images
Interior Photos: Shutterstock Images, 4–5, 14, 22; Nigel Baker Photography/Shutterstock Images, 6; Vasyl Syniuk/Shutterstock Images, 9; Sozina Kseniia/Shutterstock Images, 10; Martin of Sweden/Shutterstock Images, 12–13; Marie Charouzova/Shutterstock Images, 15; Uzo Borewicz/Shutterstock Images, 17; Jack Nevitt/Shutterstock Images, 18; Wave Break Media/iStockphoto, 20–21; Red Line Editorial, 24; Magnifical Productions/Shutterstock Images, 26; Christian Musat/Shutterstock Images, 28; Eric Isselee/Shutterstock Images, 29

Editor: Arnold Ringstad
Series Designer: Katharine Hale

Library of Congress Control Number: 2022949095

Publisher's Cataloging-in-Publication Data

Names: Pearson, Marie, author.
Title: Horse behavior / by Marie Pearson
Description: Minneapolis, Minnesota: Abdo Publishing Company, 2024 | Series: Animal behavior | Includes online resources and index.
Identifiers: ISBN 9781098291037 (lib. bdg.) | ISBN 9781098277215 (ebook)
Subjects: LCSH: Horses--Behavior--Juvenile literature. | Horses--Juvenile literature. | Mammalogy--Juvenile literature.
Classification: DDC 591.51--dc23

CONTENTS

Horses that are happy may play with each other.

CHAPTER 1

Horseplay

Zoey and her friend Steve leaned over the fence of the horse **pasture**. Steve's family lived on a farm. They had five horses. Zoey had never met a horse up close before!

Friendly horses may bite each other playfully.

Zoey spotted three horses **grazing** nearby. Suddenly, a brown horse came racing from the far side of the field. His hooves thudded on the ground. He ran toward a gray horse. The two horses circled each other. They snapped their teeth. They kicked at the air and **reared**. Then they took off running side by side.

Zoey asked, "Why are they fighting?"

"They aren't fighting, they're playing!" Steve said. He explained that if they were fighting, their ears would have been flattened back against their necks. They would have looked tense. And they would have bitten and kicked hard. But these horses had a loose, bouncy movement. They were only biting and kicking at the air.

The two horses ran around a bit more. Then they settled down and started munching grass. Zoey decided they were the most beautiful animals she had ever seen.

Horse Communication

Knowing what a horse is thinking and feeling is important for interacting with them. It helps

Safe to Play?

Because horses are so large, gentle play for them could cause serious injury to a person. So most people do not play directly with horses. Instead, they give their horses toys such as large balls. They also make sure their horses have other horse friends to play with.

Caring for horses is a lot of work, but it can be very rewarding.

people give horses the care they need, such as veterinary care. It also keeps people safe. Horses can weigh up to 2,000 pounds (900 kg). They can easily harm a person.

Knowing how to read a horse's body language can reveal how the horse is feeling.

Horses communicate mainly through body language. The positions of their eyes, ears, heads, tails, and more give clues about horses' feelings. So do the sounds a horse makes. Understanding what a horse is saying helps both horse and human build trust.

Explore Online

Visit the website below. Does it give any new information about horse behavior that wasn't in Chapter One?

Understanding Your Horse's Body Language

abdocorelibrary.com/horse-behavior

Along with other signs of relaxation, a calm horse may cock its leg, resting only the edge of a hoof on the ground.

CHAPTER 2

Understanding the Horse

Horses live in groups called herds. The horses in a herd communicate with one another. This helps everyone get along and stay safe.

A calm horse has a relaxed neck, tail, and nostrils. It has soft eyes. Its lower lip may droop.

A horse with soft eyes is feeling calm.

The ears are loosely pricked up, facing forward or outward. Horses sometimes nicker to greet each other. A nicker is a soft rumbling sound. A mother may do this when she greets her foal. A relaxed horse may cock one back leg. Only the front edge of one hoof touches the ground, and most of the weight is supported by the other legs.

Sometimes things around a horse catch its attention. The horse becomes curious and alert.

An alert horse points its ears toward whatever it has noticed.

Its ears are pricked forward at whatever has its attention. Its body is tense. The horse may decide to relax after a while. Or it may become nervous.

Keeping Safe

Horses are **prey** animals. They are always watchful for animals that might hunt them. This means that horses become scared more easily than **predators** such as dogs. A worried horse's legs are ready to run. Its neck is raised, and its back is tense. Its ears are focused forward. The jaw is tight, and its nostrils **flare**. The horse may snort. Its eyelids are tense and wrinkled.

Easily Spooked

Horses can spook at things that seem harmless to people. Plastic bags, spray bottles, and even the wind can startle a horse. For horses, being alert and running away from possible danger are important for staying alive and not getting eaten.

A spooked horse is alert and ready to escape danger.

A horse may become nervous if it is separated from another horse. It will **whinny** to try to help the horse find its way back. In a very scared horse, the whites of its eyes will show.

Horses will first try to run away from a threat. But if they feel trapped, they may try to protect themselves. A horse often gives some signs that it may strike. Its ears flatten back. Its jaw clenches, and there are creases around its nose.

If one horse does not back down, horses may fight.

Its tail swishes quickly. It may stomp or raise a back leg as a warning that it could kick. As a last resort, a horse may bite or **strike** with a front hoof. It might kick with its back hooves.

Other horses can do things to reduce the tension. They will move away from the aggressive horse. They will lower their heads, tuck their tails against their rumps, and turn away.

Primary Source

Wendy Williams is a science journalist who rides horses. She explained one reason horses need to communicate with each other:

> If a predator, for example, appears on the horizon, one horse immediately alerts the others through a wide variety of signals. Snorting, pricked ears, and stamping are only a few of these signals.

Source: Barbara J. King. "How Smart Are Horses?" *NPR*, 12 Jan. 2017, npr.org. Accessed 2 Sept. 2022.

Comparing Texts

Think about the quote. Does it support the information in this chapter or give a different perspective? Explain how in a few sentences.

Veterinarians can help a horse if it needs medical attention.

CHAPTER 3

Caring for Horses

Learning how horses communicate is important when caring for them. If a horse's behavior changes, it may mean the horse is sick or in pain. For example, a horse may become less energetic. Or it may lose interest in food or water.

Spending time with horses can help reduce boredom for the animals.

Boredom causes some noticeable behaviors. A bored horse may chew the wood of its stall. Or it may swing its head back and forth, shifting its weight from one front leg to the other.

Owners can help by riding these horses more and giving them more pasture time with other horses.

Good Interactions

Knowing how horses behave also helps keep people safe around horses. People should know when a horse is telling them to move away. They should back off before a horse feels it needs to protect itself. Some horses have learned that they can get their way if they bite, kick, or strike out. A trainer may be needed.

People should watch a horse's body language before they try to approach it. A horse that is happy and relaxed might not be paying attention to its surroundings.

Horse Vision

Knowing where a horse's blind spots are can help a person safely approach the animal.

It's important to get the horse's attention before walking up to it. Otherwise, it could startle and accidentally hurt the person.

Horses can see almost entirely around their bodies. But they have two blind spots. One is directly in front of their heads. The other is straight behind them. People shouldn't approach a horse in its blind spots. The horse may run away. Or it might get scared and kick the person. Approaching the horse's shoulder is best.

Desensitizing a Horse

Trainers desensitize horses to make them less likely to spook. They slowly show the horse new things that could scare it. This teaches the horse that these things aren't a threat. For example, people may place objects such as flags on the pasture fencing. The horse learns that things flapping and making noise aren't dangerous.

Knowing how horses behave is key in forming a strong bond between animal and owner.

Training also helps people and horses stay safe. Before a horse is ridden, people spend a lot of time desensitizing the horse. This means getting it used to sights, sounds, and smells that could spook it. Doing this makes a horse safer to be around.

Horses are very large. They can be dangerous. But many people and horses have close relationships. They trust each other. Understanding horse behavior is important so that both can feel safe and loved.

Further Evidence

Look at the website below. Does it give any new evidence to support Chapter Three?

Safe Horse Handling

abdocorelibrary.com/horse-behavior

Body Language

Relaxed

Nervous

Glossary

flare
to open wide

grazing
eating grasses

pasture
an enclosed grassy area for animals to graze

predator
an animal that hunts and eats other animals

prey
animals that are hunted by other animals

reared
stood up on the back legs

strike
when a horse kicks forward with its front feet

whinny
a gentle neighing noise made by a horse

Online Resources

To learn more about horse behavior, visit our free resource websites below.

Core Library CONNECTION
FREE! COMMON CORE MULTIMEDIA RESOURCES

Visit **abdocorelibrary.com** or scan this QR code for free Common Core resources for teachers and students, including vetted activities, multimedia, and booklinks, for deeper subject comprehension.

Booklinks NONFICTION NETWORK
FREE! ONLINE NONFICTION RESOURCES

Visit **abdobooklinks.com** or scan this QR code for free additional online weblinks for further learning. These links are routinely monitored and updated to provide the most current information available.

Learn More

Mills, Andrea. *The Everything Book of Horses and Ponies.* DK, 2019.

Smith, Robyn. *Horse Life.* Rockridge, 2020.

Ventura, Marne. *Horses.* Abdo, 2023.

Index

About the Author

Marie Pearson is a children's book author and editor. She spends her free time learning about animal behavior and training. She has always loved horses and took riding lessons as a kid.